CAMERACOLOUR PORTRAIT

Cinque Ports

Photographs and Text by
OLIVER MATHEWS

Town County BOOKS

A Member of the Ian Allan Group of Companies

First published 1984

ISBN 0 86364 019 2

Photographs © Oliver Mathews

Published by Town & County Books Ltd, Shepperton, Surrey;
and printed by Ian Allan Printing
at their works at Coombelands, Runnymede, England

INTRODUCTION

For as long as there has been any kind of civilisation in the British Isles by far the greater part of all England's communications with the continent of Europe have been through the far southeastern corner of the country. Commercially, militarily, spiritually, the southeast has been the key to the nation: Julius Caesar landed here in 55 and 54 BC; the Jutes, the Saxons and Vikings all came this way; St Augustine too, in 597 AD, when he brought Christianity to southern England; and, as everybody knows, William the Conqueror landed near Pevensey before moving on to defeat Harold at the Battle of Hastings in 1066. Then, all through the early Middle Ages as trade and prosperity increased, the French made savage, fleeting raids on the ports of this stretch of coast line. Later in history, of course, Napoleon had his eye on the same area; and even in this present 20th century Hitler entertained similar thoughts.

So it was that at a very early date in history the people who lived and worked in this part of the world were of necessity drawn together — at first probably for their own merchant interest and then soon after, no doubt, for the security of their fellow countrymen. It seems that well before the Norman Conquest there was an arrangement

Below:
The remains of St Mary's Church and the Roman lighthouse in Dover Castle. An engraved illustration to Edward Hasted's *History of Kent*, 1790.

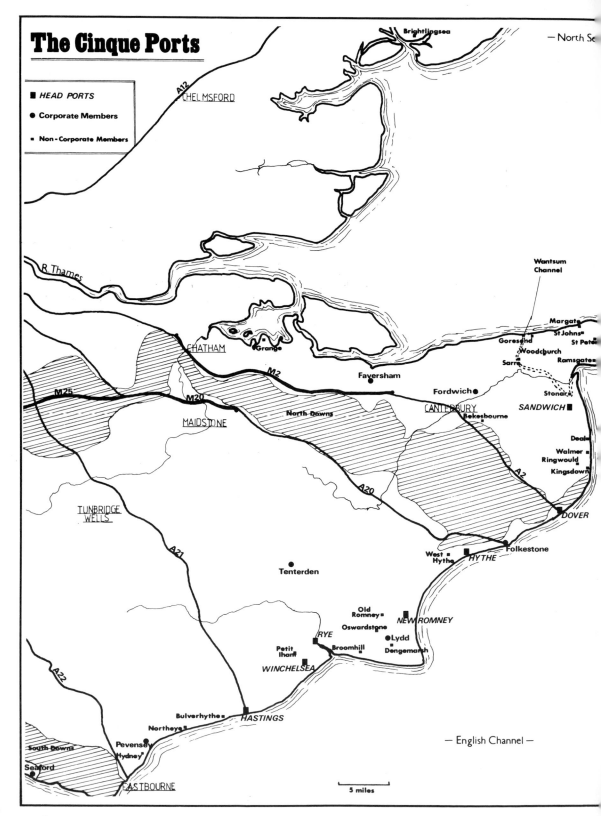

The Cinque Ports

■ *HEAD PORTS*

● Corporate Members

▪ Non-Corporate Members

Brightlingsea

— North Se

A12

CHELMSFORD

R. Thames

Wantsum Channel

Margate

St Johns

St Peter

Goresend

Woodchurch

Ramsgate

CHATHAM

Grange

Sarre

M2

Faversham

Fordwich

Stonar

M25

M20

CANTERBURY

SANDWICH

MAIDSTONE

North Downs

Bekesbourne

Deal

Walmer

Ringwould

Kingsdown

A2

A20

TUNBRIDGE WELLS

DOVER

A21

West Hythe

HYTHE

Folkestone

Tenterden

Old Romney

NEW ROMNEY

Oswardstone

RYE

Lydd

Broomhill

Dengemarsh

Petit Iham

WINCHELSEA

A22

Bulverhythe

HASTINGS

Northeye

South Downs

Pevensey

Hydney

Seaford

EASTBOURNE

— English Channel —

5 miles

4

whereby the larger, richer ports supplied ships and services to this end, and out of such an arrangement there evolved the Confederation of Cinque Ports — the first foundations of England's maritime power. (Rather confusingly, the 'correct pronunciation' of the word Cinque in this context is we are told 'sink'.)

Above:
Faversham. Drawn by T. M. Baynes and engraved by H. Adlard, 1830.

Below:
Fishergate, Sandwich. Drawn by W. Tombleson and engraved by J. Greig, 1819, for *Excursions in the County of Kent*, 1822.

The original five were Hastings, New Romney, Hythe, Dover and Sandwich, and although two or three of them had received individual royal charters in the 12th century, it is believed that their first charter granted to them as a corporate body was that issued by Edward I in 1278.

Briefly, this first charter from King Edward and those that followed from different monarchs over the four succeeding centuries requested of the ports that when called upon they provided a specific number of ships (up to 57) and as many seamen as was necessary to man each one for the service of the king and defence of the country; at their own expense for up to 15 days a year, and at the expense of the Crown for any days thereafter. In return the ports and their citizens were granted special privileges which in practice amounted to little short of self-government, with the right to hold their own courts, the exemption from national taxes, and the freedom of trade wherever they wished.

Another privilege, known as 'Den and Strond', gave them the opportunity to gain for themselves what must have been a lion's share of the North Sea herring fishery by allowing them, with their probably larger and better boats, to land and sell their catches free of charge on the shore at Great Yarmouth. Furthermore, they were given the right to run the annual Yarmouth Fair associated with the herring fishing. Not surprisingly such an arrangement in favour of outsiders aroused a fair amount of ill-will, and history records at least one bloody battle between the Cinque Portsmen and the Great Yarmouth fishermen, with considerable loss of life and vessel. Tradition has it that the

Below:
Barons of the Cinque Ports bearing the royal canopy at the coronation of King James II in 1685.

Cinque Portsmen were zealous to a fault in the exercise of their privileges, extracting as much benefit as they could, and maybe a bit more besides, from every one. One of the banners used in past Yarmouth Fairs hangs today in the Council Chamber and Court Room of the Maison Dieu, Dover. It shows the arms of the Cinque Ports: three gold lions halved and joined to three silver ships' sterns, on a halved red and blue ground.

Prima facie, a less contentious privilege was that granted to Barons of the Cinque Ports, as their senior freemen were known, to support the canopy over the king and queen of England at every coronation. Even here though, particularly in later dates when the ports' power was on the wane and other bodies had their eyes on the honour, it is said that undignified scuffles accompanied by provocative pushing and pulling broke out at more than one coronation.

As the original five became richer and more powerful, availing themselves of their rights and privileges, and as their responsibilities became more burdensome, they were joined at various times by over 30 other town and village ports. These were known as the 'Limbs' of the 'Head Port' to which they were attached. Foremost among these were the two 'Ancient Towns' of Rye and Winchelsea which began their association with the confederation as limbs of Hastings before becoming head ports in their own right.

The limbs were classed either as corporate or non-corporate members, and they enjoyed many of the privileges as well as contributing to the responsibilities of their seniors. Corporate members naturally played greater parts than non-corporate, although in several cases, with changing fortunes and circumstances, some may have surpassed others in importance.

The list of Cinque Ports most generally quoted is that embodied in the 1668 charter of King Charles II. It is as follows:

Head Ports	Corporate Members	Non-corporate Members
HASTINGS	Seaford Pevensey	Hydney Northeye Bulverhythe Petit Iham Bekesbourne Grange
NEW ROMNEY	Lydd	Broomhill Oswardstone Old Romney Dengemarsh
HYTHE	—	West Hythe
DOVER	Folkestone Faversham	Kingsdown Ringwould St Peter's St John's Margate Goresend Woodchurch
SANDWICH	Fordwich	Walmer Deal Stonar Ramsgate Sarre Brightlingsea
WINCHELSEA	—	—
RYE	Tenterden	—

It will be seen from this list that the ports concerned ran right round the coasts of present day East Sussex and Kent, from Seaford to Grange, and that there was in addition the one small haven of Brightlingsea on the Essex coast.

The heyday of the Cinque Ports was probably that period of some 200 years from the middle of the 12th century, right through the 13th century and into the first half of the 14th century. Militarily it was the time of trouble with France, and of one raid after another by the French upon towns like Rye and Winchelsea, Hastings and Sandwich, in fact it seems that no town along the coast was safe for long from the plundering Frenchmen. But such raids earned sharp retaliation, revenge and probably more as well, from the fiery portsmen. In religious affairs it was a time of disagreements between church and crown: in 1164 Thomas à Becket departed from Sandwich for six years of exile; it was shortly after his return through the

same port in 1170 that he was murdered in Canterbury Cathedral. His four killers were said to have made the final plans for their deed in Saltwood Castle, just inland from Hythe, the night before and in total darkness so as not to see each other's faces.

Commercially this was the period when much of southern England's prosperity was built up on wool, both as a raw material and as the manufactured cloth, with the Cinque Ports handling most of the trade. But there were heavy taxes on the export of one and the import of the other, as high quality English wool was much in demand by northern European weavers, whose finished cloth in return was highly prized in England; and, if the history books are to be believed, the ports — even allowing for their exemption from many taxes and other privileges — could still not resist the temptation to indulge in some smuggling. They are said too to have not been at all averse to a bit of wrecking and piracy, and while these may have been suppressed with the passage of time, smuggling in this corner of England continued well into the 16th, 17th and 18th centuries, maybe even later, when wool and

Below:
Ypres Tower, Rye. Engraved by Newton, 1785.

cloth were not the only commodities in which the 'gentlemen' took an interest.

Under their various charters the Cinque Ports and their limbs took up their rights to self administration and justice through their own Court of Shepway — the Lathe of Shepway was the Saxon name for most of the modern county of Kent. It is thought that this court was held just outside the village of Lympne and the point is marked by a commemorative cross erected in 1923. In addition there were the two smaller courts of Brodhull and Guestling — the former is thought to have taken its name from a lost hamlet in or near Dymchurch, while the latter was probably named after the village of Guestling near Hastings. The Court of Brodhull dealt with such matters of privilege as the Great Yarmouth herring fishery, and the Court of Guestling was concerned with affairs touching directly upon the ports of Hastings, Rye and Winchelsea, and their limbs. In the later years of the Cinque Ports' history these two were generally held at New Romney, combined under the partly corrupted title of The Courts of Brotherhood and Guestling.

The Court of Shepway was presided over by the Lord Warden of the Cinque Ports, a post which was once one of the most powerful and influential in the land, but since the decline in importance of the confederation, and in more recent times, it has become something of a sinecure — albeit one that is still highly respected. Later holders of the office have included William Pitt the Younger, the first Duke of Wellington, Sir Winston Churchill, Sir Robert Menzies and, at the present time, Her Majesty Queen Elizabeth the Queen Mother.

William Pitt's term of office, from 1792 to 1805, coincided with the Napoleonic Wars and the threat of a major invasion from France. During this period, and largely under the direction of William Pitt, the Military Canal was cut across the northern limits of Romney Marsh from Hythe to Winchelsea, while at the same time, all along the coast from Folkestone to Seaford a whole string of Martello Towers were hastily thrown up.

Below:
Lympne Castle. Drawn and etched by F. W. L. Stockdale, 1810, for *Forty Etchings in Kent*, 1811.

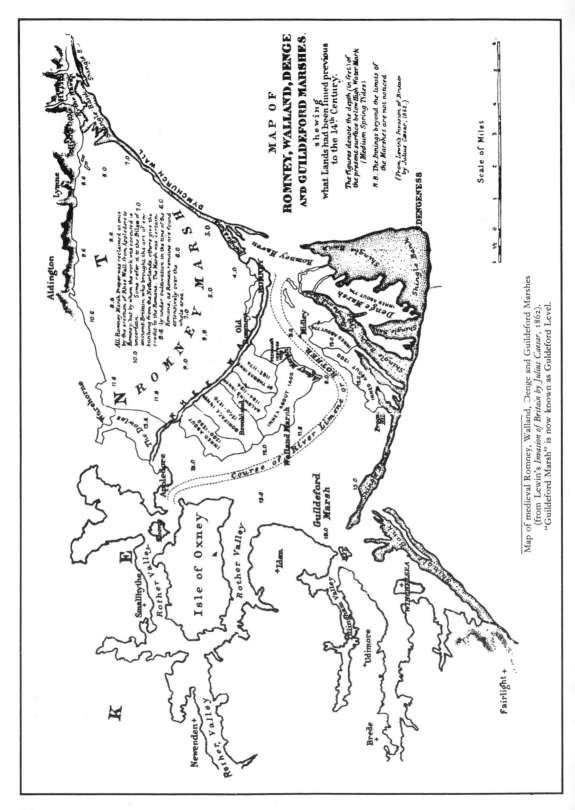

Map of medieval Romney, Walland, Denge and Guildeford Marshes
(from Lewin's *Invasion of Britain by Julius Caesar*, 1862).
"Guildeford Marsh" is now known as Guildeford Level.

Many of these round, slightly tapering towers built like primitive inverted bucket sand-castles are still standing, and although unconnected to the ports' own period of power as a confederation they are very much a part of the area's history, and serve as further illustration of the vulnerability of the southeastern coast. The Martello Towers may be regarded, in one way, as a con-tinuation of the original prime purpose of the Cinque Ports Confederation.

The decline of the Ports as a maritime power from the mid-14th century onwards was brought about by two inter-related factors, both of them outside the control of the confederation. Firstly the changing ways of warfare made it necessary for the monarch of the day, whether of aggressive or defen-sive intent, to maintain a more permanent and considerably larger marine force, larger in both size and numbers of vessels. The Cinque Ports inability to provide these newer and larger ships was the result in part at least of the second main reason for their decline — the silting up or erosion of their harbours.

Since the 11th century the coast line of southeast England has undergone several significant alterations brought about by a combination of strong 'eastward drift' of shingle in the English Channel and the ravages of the wind and water — particularly during a series of devastating storms in the 13th century, culminating in the Great Storm of 1287. Because of these changes many of the towns and villages were left some con-siderable distance from any navigable access to the sea: their development and prosperity suffered accordingly.

Before the twin movements of shingle and silt, for instance, Thanet was in fact a true sea-surrounded island, separated from the rest of Kent by the Wantsum Channel. This flowed from Reculver in the north to Sandwich in the east: a natural, sheltered waterway that allowed several small ports

along the way to build up a not insignificant merchant existence — places like Sarre and Fordwich — particularly Fordwich, the port for Canterbury. But the elements changed all that and over a period of time the Wantsum Channel silted up to leave all such places high and dry. Ultimately even Sandwich, which had probably surpassed London as the chief port of the land, was forced into decline as the channel ceased to provide sufficient water for ships of any size to come and go as they wished.

On the south coast of Kent and Sussex wind and water wrought similar changes, not least upon New Romney and Winchelsea. It is nowadays quite hard to imagine New Romney as a major port, but such indeed was the case 800 years ago when the town stood on the edge of a natural harbour sheltered from the English Channel by a broad bank of shingle. But silting up was already in pro-

gress, and its very near neighbour, Old Romney, had probably been abandoned as a port for some years when the 13th century storms broke through the protective bank causing deep flooding in New Romney and leaving behind them a depth of silt and shingle so that it too was rendered ineffective as a working port.

To talk of Winchelsea in connection with the Cinque Ports is to talk not so much about the present small town on a hill just west of Rye, but more about the original Winchelsea which it is believed lay two or three miles to the south at a point now beneath the sea where it was completely overwhelmed by the storm of 1287 — houses, church, harbour, everything. Yet the town was of such strategic value that the king of the day, Edward I, ordered a replacement to be built on high ground farther inland, and it is this grid-planned medieval town that is the Winchelsea of today. Although even here on

the hill, the 'new' Winchelsea's surrounding seas silted up with the passage of time, to leave behind the pleasant but not sufficiently navigable River Brede.

Farther round the coast, Hastings was the victim of erosion rather than silt and the original port's sea defences were washed away on several different occasions. All attempts to rebuild have come to very little and the town's once famous harbour has it seems gone for ever. But not its fishing

activities, and the fishing boats of Hastings drawn up on the shingle Stade immediately below the black boarded net lofts provide one of the most picturesque sights of the whole south coast.

Pevensey and Seaford, were the two main limbs of Hastings, but neither is a port any longer. Pevensey suffered a similar fate as New Romney, and Seaford, once a port of no mean proportions at the mouth of the Sussex Ouse, was left stranded after another great storm in the 16th century and the river's line was changed to join the sea at a point that is now Newhaven. What Newhaven is today, Seaford might have been — for better or worse.

So though the original Cinque Ports and their limbs have lost much of their great maritime power they are still bound together in origin and historic association, and in being so they maintain the name of an organisation that in its time was as important as any in the British Isles; an organisation on which was built the national navy; and one that is a milepost in the history of these islands.

For these reasons alone it is rewarding to look at the ports today both individually and corporately. In several cases little or nothing of their early involvement with the con-federation will be immediately recognisable, as besides the changes through nature and navy already discussed, other customs have changed with the passage of time — modern leisure activities tend to overrun the traditional seafaring and fishing ways of living. Yet seen in the light of their great period, and in the light of the centuries that followed when the enterprise and character of their citizens continued to create new townscapes, fine new buildings, houses and terraces, right up to the 20th century, then the picture they present reflects something of the very essence of English life across a thousand years.

Left:
The entrance to Hastings from the London Road. Lithograph by R. Martin after T. Ross, *circa* 1850.

Hastings — Fishing boats on The Stade. The original Hastings harbour was washed away in the great storms of the 13th century, and although repeated attempts were made to build a wall-protected haven right up to the late 19th century not one met with any measure of success. But the remains of the last effort still provide a rough breakwater for the row of fishing boats pulled up on the shingle below the old town — boats mostly medium-size and small, wood built, and with names like *Our Pam & Peter*, *Our Lady*, *Two Brothers* and *St Richard*, tended by their owners, surrounded by fishing equipment, nets and floats, lobster pots and, not so attractive, discarded fish guts.

It is a scene that can have changed hardly at all for several centuries: a few items of equipment may be more modern, but the essential spirit of the picture is probably much the same as it would have been in the early Middle Ages after the harbour was destroyed.

Hastings — Preparing a new net by the fishermen's lofts. The black weatherboarded fishermen's lofts built on the shingle immediately above the fishing boats of Hastings are a unique architectural phenomenon. Mostly tall and slender, of rectangular section and with pitch roofs, they date from the 16th or 17th centuries — maybe earlier. One glance inside any open door will confirm that their use continues the same as ever, even though man made fibres, like those being used to prepare the gill net in this photograph, are replacing the old materials. Certainly the huts are exactly the same as in the mid-19th century when Francis Frith came here for his book *The Gossiping Photographer at Hastings* and found 'a unique collection of large black wooden boxes, or small black warehouses, which hold the nets, tackle, and other "findings" of the 60 fishing smacks consituting the fleet of this chief of the Cinque Ports'.

18

Hastings Castle. Hastings Castle is one of a number of fortifications in southern England that the Normans built or adapted following their conquest of the country in 1066. But today at Hastings little remains beyond a few picturesque ruins looking out to sea from the top of West Hill.

Below the castle, on one side of West Hill is the old part of the town, and on the other two, to the west and north, there is the comparatively modern Hastings — a town that developed as a seaside resort from the early 19th century. The late Regency Pelham Crescent, just underneath the castle, was one of the first schemes in this development and, as such, a herald of the satellite town of St Leonard's designed by James and Decimus Burton in the late 1820s.

The growth of Hastings continued throughout the 19th century and right up to the present time, with such seaside 'pleasures' as amusement arcades and beach fair grounds — although the Central Cricket Ground and the International Hastings Chess Congress go some way towards maintaining a balance.

Hastings — Old houses by St Clement's Church. Inland from the fishing boats and net lofts the old town of Hastings leads up the valley between the East and West Hills, with St Clement's Church just off the High Street on one side, and All Saints' Church towards the top on the other.

Along the High Street and All Saints' Street, and up the small by-ways in between, there are a great many small houses of historic interest and character. Of these, *Dickens Cottage* and *Shovells*, very small, timber-framed houses, are among the oldest — *Shovells* is 'ye reputed home' of the mother of Sir Cloudesley Shovell, 17th and early 18th century admiral.

Hastings' artistic and literary associations are many and varied. They range from Byron and Keats, to Edward Lear and Holman Hunt, D. G. Rossetti and Elizabeth Siddal, all of who stayed or lived in or around Hastings at different points in their careers. But less often mentioned is Robert Tressell (the pseudonym of Robert Noonan) who lived and worked in the town as a sign writer and house decorator at the turn of this century, and whose book *The Ragged Trousered Philanthropists*, based on the town of 'Mugsborough' — in fact Hastings — is said to have influenced the development of socialism in this country.

Seaford — St Leonard's Church.
Originally the Sussex River Ouse
followed a line through the South
Downs that brought it out into
Seaford Bay somewhere just
below St Leonard's Church in the
centre of Seaford. At this point
there was a port of sufficient size
to justify Seaford's corporate
membership of the Cinque Ports
as a limb of Hastings. And
Seaford might well have stayed a
port to this day, having survived,
perhaps benefited from, the great
Channel storms of the 13th
century. But in 1579 yet another
storm finally brought with it a
change in the course of the river
which then took the shortest way
to the sea and emerged some
two miles to the west, at the
hamlet of Meeching — now
Newhaven.

Traces of Norman work in
St Leonard's Church indicate the
early date of this surprisingly
large, sculptural church which
has been added to and
embellished through most of the
succeeding centuries — the
tower in particular has some
good 15th century flint and stone
check pattern work.

Pevensey Castle. The Romans built the first very large enclosure of Pevensey Castle, in or around the 4th century AD, and when William the Conqueror landed in Pevensey Bay, some 700 years later, an easily navigable tidal creek came right up to the Roman walls where a small port was built. In this capacity Pevensey became a corporate member of the Cinque Ports as a limb of Hastings.

Within the walls of the Roman castle, the Normans then built their own moated keep, and it is the well-kept ruins of this that are the centre of interest today — as sheep graze the outer confines of the earlier Roman building. Of interest too in Pevensey, in the village, are the diminutive old Court House *cum* Town Hall, and the old Mint House — indications that Pevensey was once a port and town of considerable importance before, like so many other Cinque Ports, the harbour became choked with silt and sand.

26

Rye. Whilst a receding sea has left Rye some two miles inland, the River Rother is still easily navigable for small ships right up to the foot of the town where a fleet of fishing boats come alongside their fragile, net-laden wooden jetties. Behind them the parish church of St Mary the Virgin dominates the skyline of the 'ancient town'.

Rye was one of the many south coast ports to fall victim to the raids of marauding Frenchmen during the 14th century. But these were invariably returned with interest, and on one occasion the people of Rye managed to regain the church bells carried off by the French a few years earlier, in a raid that left the church very badly damaged. St Mary's, as it now stands, dates basically from the rebuilding that followed the raid.

Possessed of a past steeped in seafaring and all kinds of adventuring, stories of violence are part of the history of Rye; stories that include the murder of one Allen Grebell in 1743 by John Breads, a butcher, who had mistaken him for the mayor, James Lamb, against whom he bore a long standing grudge. Breads was subsequently hanged, and the remains of his gibbet-chained skull are still to be seen in the Town Hall — a handsome, 18th century neo-classical building, colonnaded at street level.

The Lamb family provided a string of local mayors in the 18th and 19th centuries and Lamb House, built by James Lamb in the early 18th century, is one of the most interesting houses in the town with strong literary associations — especially round the names of Henry James and E. F. Benson who lived there in the early part of this century.

Rye — The Mermaid Inn. With cobbled streets and interesting buildings, history and associations on every hand, Rye today presents a near perfect image of a small English market town and port — a cliché perhaps, but nonetheless true.

Church Square, Market Street and Watchbell Street all have fine early houses in a mixture of materials, timber, stone, brick and hung tile. While Church Square also has the 13th century fortification, Ypres Tower, in one corner, and, just by the church, the very unusual 18th century Water House — a brick built oval over an underground tank into which the town's water was pumped up from the bottom of the hill. But Mermaid Street is the best known of all, not least because of the Mermaid Inn, a good timber frame building dating mostly from the 15th century, with a colourful history much intertwined with smuggling — the notorious 18th century 'Hawkhurst Gang' are said to have openly celebrated their successes at the windows of the inn overlooking the street.

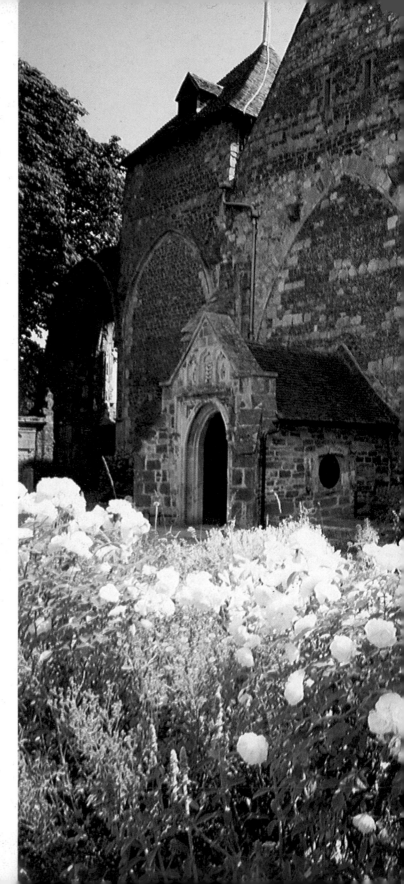

Winchelsea — St Thomas's Church. The first Winchelsea was completely overwhelmed in the great Channel storms of the 13th century, and sank beneath the sea. It is believed to have lain some two or three miles to the southeast of the present town, and as such was probably strategically very important to the security of southern England — so much so that Edward I took a particular interest in having a replacement built soon after the original had become untenable. This was designed to a regular grid pattern, and, in view of the distance between the centre of the town and New Gate — nearly a mile away amongst trees and fields — it was probably intended to be much larger than it actually turned out. Nonetheless Winchelsea is one of the most attractive and quietest of small towns and has towards the centre the church of St Thomas the Martyr of Canterbury. This fine building was severely damaged in a series of raids by the French during the 14th century; and these raids are generally thought to account for the fact that only the east end is still standing. Of particular interest inside is the tomb of Gervase Alard which has sculpted portrait heads of Queen Margaret and Edward I supporting the decorative canopy.

Outside, beyond the missing west end of the church, a tree marks the spot where John Wesley preached his last open air sermon in 1790.

Smallhythe Place, near Tenterden. Before the coast of southeast England was so altered by storm and silt, and even up to the 18th century, Smallhythe — then on a broad reach of the River Rother passing north of the Isle of Oxney — was the not inconsiderable port at Tenterden, just two miles away. Through this port, and the town's own wealth as a Wealden cloth town, Tenterden became a corporate member of the Cinque Ports as a limb of Rye in 1449.

Besides serving as Tenterden's port, Smallhythe is known to have maintained a shipbuilding industry over a period of several centuries; and even as late as the 16th century quite large ships were still being built here.

Smallhythe Place, originally the Port Officer's house overlooking the harbour, is a very fine 15th century timber frame house in an excellent state of preservation. During the first quarter of the century it was the home of the actress Helen Terry, and now owned by the National Trust it houses a small collection of theatrical memorabilia.

Smallhythe declined rapidly as a port after a silted River Rother was diverted to the south of Oxney in the 18th century.

Old Romney — St Clement's Church. Even as early as 1278 — the date of the first corporate royal charter of the Cinque Ports — Old Romney had probably already lost much of its importance as a port through the then gradual processes of silting up of its waterway and land reclamation in Romney Marsh. But as a limb of New Romney, scarcely two miles away, the town or port — to use such words to describe this lovely but very small place hardly seems appropriate — must still have been sufficiently active in maritime affairs to justify membership of the confederation, even though this was only at the non-corporate level.

The Old Romney of today is little more than a small handful of scattered houses, mostly of an early date, in the vicinity of St Clement's church.
St Clement's itself has a Norman nave, a 14th century tower and font, an 18th century musicians' gallery and a most unusual 17th century primitive staircase to the tower for which the steps were made from great triangular sections of solid oak, rough hewn from the tree.

Outside, sheep graze round the walls of the church and under the nearby willows where once were the wharves and quays of a busy port.

Hythe — Fishing boats and Martello Towers on The Stade.
As one of the original five head ports of the confederation, Hythe was obviously a port of some consequence when the Cinque Ports were at the height of their power in the 12th, 13th and 14th centuries. But like so many others, Hythe's harbour became a victim of the inexorable process of silting up, and by the end of the 16th century, or early in the 17th, the town could no longer be called a port. Today just a few fishing boats sail from her shingle stade.

During the Napoleonic Wars Hythe was the scene of extensive military excitement: the Military Canal, a major feat of defensive engineering, was built across the northern edge of Romney Marsh, actually starting at Hythe and running right through to Winchelsea; while at the same time a series of Martello Towers were built on a longer stretch of coast line. Some of these have disappeared, but several are still standing in Hythe — two beyond the fishing boats, and one on the sea front that has been converted into a house. Their name, incidentally, is a mis-spelt derivation from Mortella in Corsica, where a similar 'prototype' first came to the attention of an English military force in the late 18th century.

Hythe — St Leonard's Church.
The main part of the old town of
Hythe stands away from the sea
and up a short, steep hill. Not far
over the top is Saltwood Castle
where Thomas à Becket's four
murderers put the finishing
touches to their evil plans before
travelling to Canterbury on the
night of 28 December 1170. Half
way up, surrounded by old
houses and looking out across
the English Channel, is the parish
church of St Leonard's — a large,
almost cathedral-sized building,
late Norman and Early English,
with a theatrically impressive
chancel, much higher than the
nave and approached by a broad
flight of steps.

Hythe's importance as a port
of any size may have long since
passed, but the town's
contribution to seafaring has
been maintained in recent times
through Lionel Lukin, who is
credited with the invention of the
lifeboat, and is buried in the
churchyard, and also through
Francis Pettit-Smith, the inventor
of the marine screw propeller,
who was born and brought up
here.

A macabre curiosity attached
to St Leonard's Church is the
extraordinary collection of skulls
and other human bones gathered
together in the ambulatory, or
crypt, below the east end. It
seems that they probably date
from the Middle Ages, but
nobody knows precisely how or
why they came to be in part of
the church.

Dover — The Eastern Docks by night. Of all the Cinque Ports, Dover is the only one that has survived the vicissitudes of centuries to remain a major international port. As the original harbour at the mouth of the River Dour silted up in the early Middle Ages, the quays and wharves were expanded beyond the confines of the creek and out into the sea where protective breakwaters and pier walls have ever since succeeded in holding back the severest seas.

Below the white cliffs and against a background of some pleasant Regency housing — Waterloo Crescent compares well with any early 19th century provincial domestic architecture — Dover Harbour currently handles nearly 14 million passengers a year, as well as $7\frac{1}{2}$ million tonnes of freight. It is the largest passenger port in the British Isles.

From the viewpoint of Langdon Cliff, it is possible to look down on the Eastern Docks, on the lines of heavy lorries, the parks of cars, newly imported or tourist applied, and on the continuous shuttle of ships — Thoresen, P&O and Sealink; all set against a cacophony of hissing hydraulic brakes, shipping announcements, engines and roar of passing hovercraft. Farther on the eye is drawn out to the main harbour breakwater, to the sea and, on any clear day, to the north coast of France. It is a strange spectacle; a kind of hypnotic whirlpool.

Dover Castle. Built on the site of extensive early Iron Age and Saxon fortifications, and standing high and clear cut on the cliffs above the town, Dover Castle dates mostly from the late 12th century and the reign of King Henry II, although further additions, notably along the outer walls, belong to the 13th century.

Henry II's inner bailey and magnificent rectangular tower keep, in Kentish rag and Caen stone, have as much strength in reality as they do in appearance. Architecturally, aesthetically correct, the keep's overall outline is that of a near perfect cube just under 100ft high, with walls between 17 and 21ft thick. Inside there are two fine spiral stone stairways, a chapel and, on a rather lower level, some interesting graffiti thought to be the handiwork of French prisoners of war. During the Napoleonic Wars the outer walls of the castle were altered and levelled in parts, primarily to provide gun emplacements; but other than this, and some minor Tudor additions, the main body of the castle has hardly changed since the end of the 13th century.

Dover Castle — the Roman Lighthouse and St Mary's Church. The Roman lighthouse, or pharos, that stands within the perimeter of Dover Castle, just next to St Mary's Church and just south of the keep and inner bailey, is thought to be the oldest building in Britain. Built in the 1st or 2nd century AD, of octagonal exterior section, and to a height probably of about 80ft, this was one of a pair of Roman lights on the cliffs above Dover — the other, no longer standing, was across the town on the Western Heights. From its strategic position above the harbour this early building has witnessed every arrival and departure for the best part of 2,000 years, including Henry VIII's extravaganza bound for the Field of the Cloth of Gold in 1520, Charles II's return to England on the restoration of the monarchy in 1660, and in the present century all the hostile activities concerned with two world wars.

Immediately next to the Roman lighthouse is the late Saxon church of St Mary in the Castle. Although extensively restored in the late 19th century a feature of the this small garrison church is the quantity of Roman materials re-used in its original construction.

Dover has a rich Roman past, and even as recently as 1970 a house built in about 200 AD with painted interior walls was discovered in the present town centre.

Folkestone — A shell fish stall on the harbour quay. Although a near neighbour of Hythe, it is perhaps particularly appropriate today that Folkestone should have become a corporate member of the Cinque Ports as a limb of Dover — the town with which it is nowadays closely associated through its activities as a cross Channel port, albeit on a very much smaller scale than Dover.

Folkestone is also a small fishing port with its own fleet of boats and fish market. Near the market are some brightly decorated stalls selling wet fish and shellfish, and jellied eels as well, for since the 19th century Folkestone has had a third life as a busy holiday resort with many of the attractions that such a description implies — including seaside entertainments in the Leas Cliff Hall. The Leas, a promenade along the cliff top backed with late 19th century hotels, houses and bandstand, still manages to echo something of its Victorian heyday.

In the old part of the town, besides the 13th century church of St Mary & St Eanswythe — the latter was the grand-daughter of King Ethelbert, first Christian king of Kent — there is an unusual old fashioned humbug shop in the High Street, where colourful sweets are made in full view of passing pedestrians.

H. G. Wells lived in Spade House on the outskirts of the town — a house built for him in 1899/1900 by C. F. Voysey. Among the books he wrote here are *The Food of the Gods, Kipps*, and *The History of Mr Polly*.

Faversham — Abbey Street.
Notwithstanding its corporate
membership of the Cinque Ports
as a limb of Dover, Faversham
has an independent air about it
that seems to transcend the
fashions of the centuries.
Standing along a narrow but
navigable creek that flows into
the River Swale, this small north
Kent town has an industrial past
and present based on gunpowder
manufacture and oyster fishing,
grain based products and
brewing — even today the
pungent, pleasant aroma of beer
in preparation pervades the
whole town.

King Stephen founded an
abbey in Faversham, where he
and Queen Matilda were
subsequently buried, but it was
destroyed during the Dissolution
of the monasteries. On the other
hand the 16th century Queen
Elizabeth Grammar School and
nearby parish church of Our Lady
of Charity, with its extraordinary
mixture of styles from Norman to
neo-classic, go some way to
redeem the loss.

Mixtures of styles, periods and
materials are a feature of
Faversham, for, besides the
church, the Guildhall has a neo-
classical upper half resting on a
16th century timber column
base; while the old houses of
Abbey Street, in their many
different forms, make up one of
the most harmonious street
scenes in England. The timber-
framed Arden House, at the end
of Abbey Street, is named after a
16th century merchant and
mayor of the town whose death
at the hands of his wife and her
lover was the inspiration of *Arden
of Faversham*, a much-praised
play of uncertain authorship. Both
Marlowe and Shakespeare have
been suggested.

Sandwich — St Clement's Church. Of Sandwich's many interesting and early buildings, whether timber framed English, Dutch influenced brick, or, more specifically, the 14th century Fishergate of 16th century Barbican, the parish church of St Clement's is surely the best of all. And undoubtedly the finest part of this great building is the Norman tower: stone built, central, four square and strong, this magnificent example of early 12th century architecture and craftsmanship has three tiers of simple, clear cut arcading to each side.

From the top of the tower the view north and west across the old houses and tiled rooftops of Sandwich stretches out over the now very small River Stour to the flat land that was once the Wantsum Channel. In the 12th, 13th and 14th centuries, when the ports were at the height of their power, this channel would have been busy with shipping passing to and from London, calling and trading at the ports in between. Farther north the view continues up to Thanet; while to the east there are the modern golf courses of Sandwich, and beyond them the sea.

Inside the church there is a 15th century octagonal font bearing the arms of the Cinque Ports, and above the door leading to the tower stairs a fine panel of decorative 12th century stonework.

Sandwich — Stained glass window in the Guildhall illustrating Queen Elizabeth I's visit to the town in 1573 (detail).
Once well placed in the southeastern end of the Wantsum Channel, Sandwich gained early prosperity in Saxon times and continued to grow in the immediately succeeding centuries to the point where, as a head Cinque Port, it probably surpassed even London in importance. During the 11th century Edward the Confessor lived in Sandwich, and during the 12th century Thomas à Becket left and returned to England through the port, whilst Richard Coeur de Lion used the same route to and from the Crusades. But then in 1287 the great storm that so devastated other harbours along the south coast, left behind it sandbanks that heralded the future silting and choking of this haven whose very name — 'haven on the sand' — suggests an uncertain longevity.

By the early 16th century, although ships still came and went, Sandwich was in trouble. Henry VIII was petitioned for assistance, so too was Queen Elizabeth, in 1558 and again in 1573 when she visited the town. At the official banquet it is said 'she was very merrye and did eat of dyvers dishes without any assaye'. Nevertheless, royal help was not forthcoming and the town's maritime life continued its decline.

The stained glass window in the Guildhall, inserted in 1907, shows the queen being greeted on her arrival. The mayor is depicted wearing brightly coloured robes, but this was purely for the one occasion as ever since an earlier mayor, John Drury, had been killed defending the town against French invaders in 1457, the mayor always wore black.

Sandwich — The Salutation.
Whilst Sandwich's prosperity and importance fell away with the decline of the Cinque Ports, the town managed to maintain a high standard of domestic architecture through the succeeding periods. Today it has a great many well-built, well-designed small and medium-sized houses of various dates. The crowning glory of this inheritance is perhaps The Salutation. Designed by Sir Edwin Lutyens in the style of the English Renaissance, this house of quite exceptional quality was built on the site of an earlier inn of the same name, just by St Clement's Church. Its excellence, in the line of English small country houses, was further enhanced by the garden which was largely the work of Gertrude Jekyll — Lutyen's frequent colleague in the art of garden making.

Within the last few years the garden has been steadily restored so that a series of broad beds of mixed herbaceous plants, a water garden and a perfect lawn now provide a colourful foreground to this particularly fine example of English domestic architecture.

Ramsgate Harbour. Ramsgate became a non-corporate member of the Cinque Ports as a limb of Sandwich, possibly at some date in the early 14th century. But over the years, as most other ports in the confederation declined, Ramsgate slowly expanded its merchant and fishing activities until in the mid-18th century a full scale stone pier-protected harbour had to be built. For the most part this was the work of John Smeaton, the engineer responsible for the first successful Eddystone Lighthouse.

Round the harbour there are several interesting buildings including an early 19th century powder magazine, a small 19th century lighthouse at the harbour entrance, an obelisk marking a visit by George IV, a dry dock also designed by John Smeaton, and the neo-Gothic Ramsgate Home for Smack Boys — a relic of the 19th century fishing industry.

During the 19th century the town's commercial prosperity further increased through its development as a seaside resort, when many of the late Regency and early Victorian houses and crescents were built overlooking the sands and sea. But in recent times, whilst this seaside trade has continued, Ramsgate's fishing fleet and merchant marine have mostly given way to a modern yacht marina and its attendant assembly of expensive pleasure boats, sail and powered, wood and plastic.

Walmer Castle. Walmer Castle was one of three small castles built by Henry VIII in 1539/40 to protect the east coast of Kent from the invasion he feared might follow his break with Rome. Of the others, Deal — like Walmer — is still in a good state of preservation, but Sandown, just over a mile farther on from Deal, is now a much reduced ruin. Built concentrically against the improved artillery of Tudor warfare, with inner keeps surrounded by rounded outer bastions, these castles were also provided with broad and deep moats.

Since the 18th century Walmer Castle has been the official residence of the Lord Warden of the Cinque Ports. As such it has strong associations with some of the later holders of the post — particularly William Pitt and the first Duke of Wellington. The Duke of Wellington especially liked Walmer, with its cannon terraces overlooking the sea, and he entertained Queen Victoria and Prince Albert here in 1842. Ten years later he died in the castle, and the room and the very chair in which he died are almost exactly as they were on that September day in 1852. Among the many interesting items displayed in the castle is a pair of his own Wellington boots.

Deal — Fishing boats along the shore. The strategic importance of Deal and Walmer is due to their positions on the east coast of Kent overlooking The Downs — that stretch of comparatively sheltered water between the mainland and the treacherous Goodwin Sands. In the days of sail there was considerable activity here as ships rode out storms or waited for favourable winds to continue their journeys. Nowadays the waters are primarily the province of small fishing boats which, when not in use, are drawn up along the shingle shore in front of the town — precisely where Julius Caesar is believed to have landed in 55 and 54 BC.

Nearby is Deal Castle, and beyond that the Time Ball Tower. This latter is a strange relic of early modern technology, between the discovery of electricity and radio, whereby a large black ball on the roof of the tower was raised just before 1pm every day and then released by direct current from Greenwich on the stroke of the hour so that the ships lying out in The Downs could set their own instruments.

Probably the oldest part of Deal is the area farther inland known as Upper Deal, surrounding St Leonard's Church, but there are many good 18th and early 19th century small houses and terraces down near the sea, particularly in and around Middle Street.

BIBLIOGRAPHY

Historic Towns: The Cinque Ports, Montagu
Burrows; Longmans, Green & Co,
2nd edition, 1888

The Seas and Shores of England, Edmund
Vale, Batsford 1936

The Cinque Ports — John Bavington Jones;
Dover Express & East Kent News,
2nd edition, 1937

The Land of the Cinque Ports, S. P. B. Mais;
Christopher Johnson, 1949

The Cinque Ports, R. F. & F. W. Jessup;
Batsford, 1952

The King's England: Sussex, Arthur Mee;
Hodder & Stoughton, 1964 edition
revised by C. L. S. Linnell

The King's England: Kent, Arthur Mee;
Hodder & Stoughton, 1969 edition
revised by C. R. Councer

The Heraldry of the Cinque Ports, Geoffrey
Williams; David & Charles, 1971

The Cinque Ports and Romney Marsh —
Margaret Brentnall; John Gifford,
enlarged edition, 1980

**List of Towns and larger Villages
Mentioned**

Hastings   3, 6, 7, 8, 9, 15, **16**, **18**, **20**, **22**
New Romney   4, 7, 13, 14
Hythe   4, 6, 7, 9, **38**, 40
Dover   3, 4, 6, 7, **42**, **44**, **46**
Sandwich   4, 5, 6, 7, 8, 11, 13, **52**, **54**, **56**
Winchelsea   4, 7, 8, 9, 13, **32**
Rye   4, 7, 8, 14, **28 30**,
Seaford   4, 7, 8, **24**
Pevensey   3, 4, 7, 15, **26**
Lydd   4, 7
Folkestone   4, 7, 11, **48**
Faversham   4, 5, 7, **50**
Tenterden   4, 7, 34
Margate   4, 7
Walmer   4, 7, **60**
Deal   4, 7, **62**
Sarre   4, 7, 13
Brightlingsea   4, 7
Fordwich   4, 7, 13
Canterbury   4, 8, 13
London   4
Great Yarmouth   6-7
Ramsgate   **58**